VIOLIN
101 DISNEY SONGS

Available for
FLUTE, CLARINET, ALTO SAX, TENOR SAX, TRUMPET,
HORN, TROMBONE, VIOLIN, VIOLA, CELLO

ISBN 978-1-5400-0240-2

The following songs are the property of:

Bourne Co.
Music Publishers
5 West 37th Street
New York, NY 10018

BABY MINE
GIVE A LITTLE WHISTLE
HEIGH-HO
HI-DIDDLE-DEE-DEE (AN ACTOR'S LIFE FOR ME)
I'M WISHING
I'VE GOT NO STRINGS
SOME DAY MY PRINCE WILL COME
WHEN I SEE AN ELEPHANT FLY
WHEN YOU WISH UPON A STAR
WHISTLE WHILE YOU WORK
WHO'S AFRAID OF THE BIG BAD WOLF?
WITH A SMILE AND A SONG

DISTRIBUTED BY

7777 W. BLUEMOUND RD. P.O. BOX 13819 MILWAUKEE, WI 53213

Visit Hal Leonard Online at
www.halleonard.com

T0019122

CONTENTS

*Based on the "Winnie the Pooh" works,
by A. A. Milne and E. H. Shepard

**TARZAN® Owned by Edgar Rice Burroughs, Inc.
and Used by Permission.
© Burroughs/Disney

BABY MINE
from DUMBO

VIOLIN

Words by NED WASHINGTON
Music by FRANK CHURCHILL

Moderately slow

THE BALLAD OF DAVY CROCKETT
from DAVY CROCKETT

Words by TOM BLACKBURN
Music by GEORGE BRUNS

Moderately

BELLA NOTTE
from LADY AND THE TRAMP

Music and Lyrics by PEGGY LEE
and SONNY BURKE

BE OUR GUEST

from BEAUTY AND THE BEAST

VIOLIN

Music by ALAN MENKEN
Lyrics by HOWARD ASHMAN

Moderately

BEAUTY AND THE BEAST

from BEAUTY AND THE BEAST

VIOLIN

Music by ALAN MENKEN
Lyrics by HOWARD ASHMAN

BELLE
from BEAUTY AND THE BEAST

VIOLIN

Music by ALAN MENKEN
Lyrics by HOWARD ASHMAN

BIBBIDI-BOBBIDI-BOO
(The Magic Song)
from CINDERELLA

Words by JERRY LIVINGSTON
Music by MACK DAVID and AL HOFFMAN

Brightly

BREAKING FREE

from HIGH SCHOOL MUSICAL

VIOLIN

Words and Music by
JAMIE HOUSTON

Moderately

BEST OF FRIENDS

from THE FOX AND THE HOUND

Violin

Words by STAN FIDEL
Music by RICHARD JOHNSTON

Moderately

CAN YOU FEEL THE LOVE TONIGHT

from THE LION KING

VIOLIN

Music by ELTON JOHN
Lyrics by TIM RICE

Pop Ballad

CANDLE ON THE WATER

from PETE'S DRAGON

Violin

Words and Music by AL KASHA
and JOEL HIRSCHHORN

Spiritually

CHIM CHIM CHER-EE

from MARY POPPINS

VIOLIN

Words and Music by RICHARD M. SHERMAN
and ROBERT B. SHERMAN

Lightly, with gusto

CIRCLE OF LIFE

from THE LION KING

VIOLIN

Music by ELTON JOHN
Lyrics by TIM RICE

Moderately (with an African beat)

THE CLIMB
from HANNAH MONTANA: THE MOVIE

VIOLIN

Words and Music by JESSI ALEXANDER
and JON MABE

Moderately slow

CRUELLA DE VIL
from 101 DALMATIANS

VIOLIN

Words and Music by
MEL LEVEN

Slow Blues

A DREAM IS A WISH YOUR HEART MAKES
from CINDERELLA

Words and Music by MACK DAVID,
AL HOFFMAN and JERRY LIVINGSTON

Moderately

FEED THE BIRDS

(Tuppence a Bag)

from MARY POPPINS

Words and Music by RICHARD M. SHERMAN
and ROBERT B. SHERMAN

COLORS OF THE WIND
from POCAHONTAS

Violin

Music by ALAN MENKEN
Lyrics by STEPHEN SCHWARTZ

DO YOU WANT TO BUILD A SNOWMAN?

from FROZEN

VIOLIN

Music and Lyrics by KRISTEN ANDERSON-LOPEZ
and ROBERT LOPEZ

DAYS IN THE SUN
from BEAUTY AND THE BEAST

VIOLIN

Music by ALAN MENKEN
Lyrics by TIM RICE

Slower

EVERMORE
from BEAUTY AND THE BEAST

VIOLIN

Music by ALAN MENKEN
Lyrics by TIM RICE

HEIGH-HO
(The Dwarfs' Marching Song)
from SNOW WHITE AND THE SEVEN DWARFS

Words by LARRY MOREY
Music by FRANK CHURCHILL

Brightly, cheerfully

FOR THE FIRST TIME IN FOREVER

from FROZEN

VIOLIN

Music and Lyrics by KRISTEN ANDERSON-LOPEZ
and ROBERT LOPEZ

Moderately, with excitement

Moderately, with expression

With excitement

With expression

HI-DIDDLE-DEE-DEE
(An Actor's Life for Me)
from PINOCCHIO

Words by NED WASHINGTON
Music by LEIGH HARLINE

Brightly, in 2

FRIEND LIKE ME

from ALADDIN

VIOLIN

Music by ALAN MENKEN
Lyrics by HOWARD ASHMAN

GASTON
from BEAUTY AND THE BEAST

VIOLIN

Music by ALAN MENKEN
Lyrics by HOWARD ASHMAN

Moderately slow, in 1

GOD HELP THE OUTCASTS

from THE HUNCHBACK OF NOTRE DAME

VIOLIN

Music by ALAN MENKEN
Lyrics by STEPHEN SCHWARTZ

GIVE A LITTLE WHISTLE
from PINOCCHIO

Words by NED WASHINGTON
Music by LEIGH HARLINE

Moderately, in 2

GO THE DISTANCE
from HERCULES

VIOLIN

Music by ALAN MENKEN
Lyrics by DAVID ZIPPEL

Slowly

HAKUNA MATATA

from THE LION KING

Violin

Music by ELTON JOHN
Lyrics by TIM RICE

Freely

Bouncy Shuffle

rall.

small notes optional

HAPPY WORKING SONG
from ENCHANTED

VIOLIN

Music by ALAN MENKEN
Lyrics by STEPHEN SCHWARTZ

HE'S A PIRATE

from PIRATES OF THE CARIBBEAN: THE CURSE OF THE BLACK PEARL

VIOLIN

Music by KLAUS BADELT,
GEOFFREY ZANELLI and HANS ZIMMER

HE'S A TRAMP
from LADY AND THE TRAMP

Words and Music by PEGGY LEE
and SONNY BURKE

Moderately

HOW DOES A MOMENT LAST FOREVER

from BEAUTY AND THE BEAST

VIOLIN

Music by ALAN MENKEN
Lyrics by TIM RICE

I JUST CAN'T WAIT TO BE KING

from THE LION KING

VIOLIN

Music by ELTON JOHN
Lyrics by TIM RICE

Bright Two-beat

HOW FAR I'LL GO

from MOANA

VIOLIN

Music and Lyrics by
LIN-MANUEL MIRANDA

Moderately, in 2

I'M LATE
from ALICE IN WONDERLAND

Words by BOB HILLIARD
Music by SAMMY FAIN

Moderately fast

I SEE THE LIGHT

from TANGLED

VIOLIN

Music by ALAN MENKEN
Lyrics by GLENN SLATER

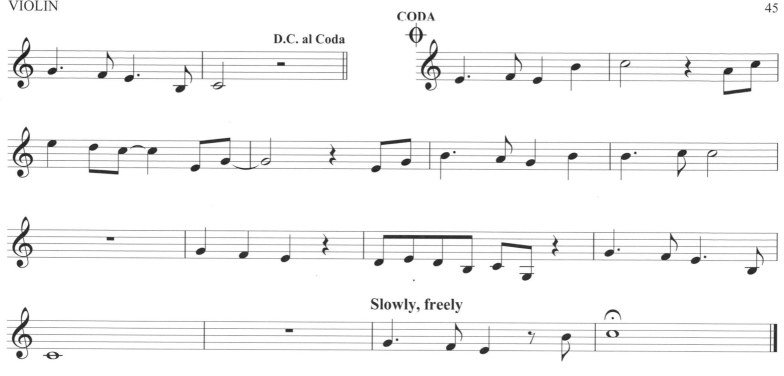

I'M WISHING

from SNOW WHITE AND THE SEVEN DWARFS

Words by LARRY MOREY
Music by FRANK CHURCHILL

I'LL MAKE A MAN OUT OF YOU
from MULAN

VIOLIN

Music by MATTHEW WILDER
Lyrics by DAVID ZIPPEL

IN SUMMER

from FROZEN

VIOLIN

Music and Lyrics by KRISTEN ANDERSON-LOPEZ
and ROBERT LOPEZ

Moderately, in 2

I'VE GOT A DREAM

from TANGLED

VIOLIN

Music by ALAN MENKEN
Lyrics by GLENN SLATER

Moderately fast

IF I CAN'T LOVE HER

from BEAUTY AND THE BEAST: THE BROADWAY MUSICAL

Violin

Music by ALAN MENKEN
Lyrics by TIM RICE

IF I NEVER KNEW YOU

(End Title)

from POCAHONTAS

VIOLIN

Music by ALAN MENKEN
Lyrics by STEPHEN SCHWARTZ

I'VE GOT NO STRINGS
from PINOCCHIO

VIOLIN

Words by NED WASHINGTON
Music by LEIGH HARLINE

Quickly, joyfully

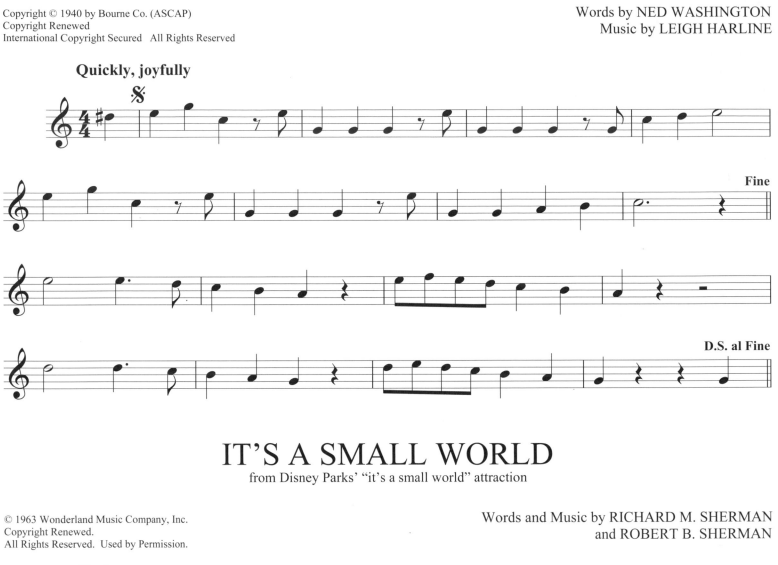

IT'S A SMALL WORLD
from Disney Parks' "it's a small world" attraction

Words and Music by RICHARD M. SHERMAN
and ROBERT B. SHERMAN

Fast

KISS THE GIRL
from THE LITTLE MERMAID

Violin

Music by ALAN MENKEN
Lyrics by HOWARD ASHMAN

LAVA
from LAVA

VIOLIN

Music and Lyrics by
JAMES FORD MURPHY

LOVE IS AN OPEN DOOR
from FROZEN

VIOLIN

Music and Lyrics by KRISTEN ANDERSON-LOPEZ
and ROBERT LOPEZ

LET IT GO
from FROZEN

VIOLIN

Music and Lyrics by KRISTEN ANDERSON-LOPEZ
and ROBERT LOPEZ

Slowly, in 2

LAVENDER BLUE
(Dilly Dilly)
from SO DEAR TO MY HEART

VIOLIN

Words by LARRY MOREY
Music by ELIOT DANIEL

MICKEY MOUSE MARCH
from THE MICKEY MOUSE CLUB

Words and Music by
JIMMIE DODD

LET'S GO FLY A KITE

from MARY POPPINS

Words and Music by RICHARD M. SHERMAN
and ROBERT B. SHERMAN

With gusto

THE LORD IS GOOD TO ME
from MELODY TIME

Words and Music by KIM GANNON
and WALTER KENT

MY FUNNY FRIEND AND ME
from THE EMPEROR'S NEW GROOVE

Lyrics by STING
Music by STING and DAVID HARTLEY

PART OF YOUR WORLD
from THE LITTLE MERMAID

VIOLIN

Music by ALAN MENKEN
Lyrics by HOWARD ASHMAN

Moderately bright

MOTHER KNOWS BEST
from TANGLED

VIOLIN

Music by ALAN MENKEN
Lyrics by GLENN SLATER

Moderately slow, in 2

A PIRATE'S LIFE
from PETER PAN

Words by ED PENNER
Music by OLIVER WALLACE

Moderately, with a bounce

RUMBLY IN MY TUMBLY
from THE MANY ADVENTURES OF WINNIE THE POOH

Words and Music by RICHARD M. SHERMAN
and ROBERT B. SHERMAN

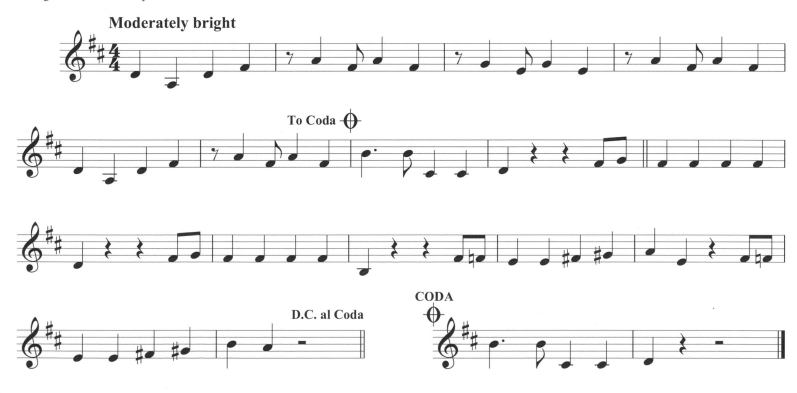

REFLECTION
from MULAN

VIOLIN

Music by MATTHEW WILDER
Lyrics by DAVID ZIPPEL

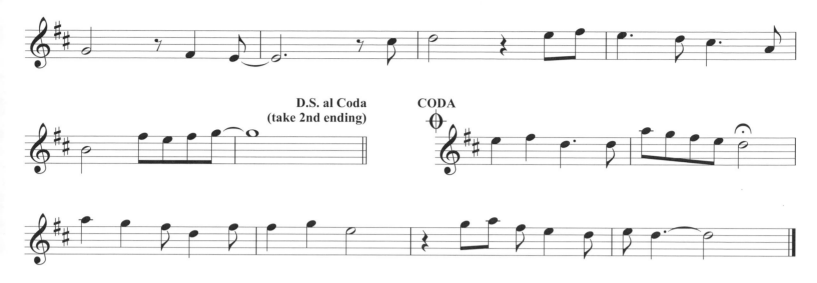

THE SECOND STAR TO THE RIGHT

from PETER PAN

Words by SAMMY CAHN
Music by SAMMY FAIN

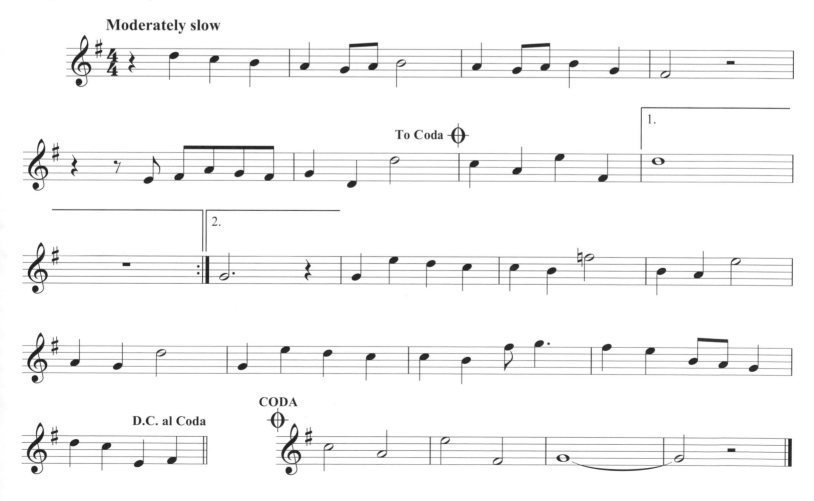

SEIZE THE DAY
from NEWSIES

VIOLIN

Music by ALAN MENKEN
Lyrics by JACK FELDMAN

SO THIS IS LOVE
from CINDERELLA

Violin

Words and Music by AL HOFFMAN,
MACK DAVID and JERRY LIVINGSTON

SO CLOSE
from ENCHANTED

VIOLIN

Music by ALAN MENKEN
Lyrics by STEPHEN SCHWARTZ

Moderately slow, in 4

Slowly, freely

THE SIAMESE CAT SONG

from LADY AND THE TRAMP

Violin

Words and Music by PEGGY LEE
and SONNY BURKE

SOME DAY MY PRINCE WILL COME

from SNOW WHITE AND THE SEVEN DWARFS

Words by LARRY MOREY
Music by FRANK CHURCHILL

SOMEDAY
from THE HUNCHBACK OF NOTRE DAME

VIOLIN

Music by ALAN MENKEN
Lyrics by STEPHEN SCHWARTZ

SOMETHING THERE

from BEAUTY AND THE BEAST

VIOLIN

Music by ALAN MENKEN
Lyrics by HOWARD ASHMAN

Moderately fast

A SPOONFUL OF SUGAR

from MARY POPPINS

Violin

Words and Music by RICHARD M. SHERMAN
and ROBERT B. SHERMAN

SUPERCALIFRAGILISTICEXPIALIDOCIOUS

from MARY POPPINS

VIOLIN

Words and Music by RICHARD M. SHERMAN
and ROBERT B. SHERMAN

Brightly

"THIS IS ME."
from RATATOUILLE

VIOLIN

Music by MICHAEL GIACCHINO

THAT'S HOW YOU KNOW
from ENCHANTED

VIOLIN

Music by ALAN MENKEN
Lyrics by STEPHEN SCHWARTZ

TOYLAND MARCH
from BABES IN TOYLAND

Adapted from V. HERBERT Melody
Words by MEL LEVEN
Music by GEORGE BRUNS

March tempo

TRASHIN' THE CAMP

(Pop Version)
from TARZAN™

VIOLIN

Words and Music by
PHIL COLLINS

THE UNBIRTHDAY SONG
from ALICE IN WONDERLAND

Violin

Words and Music by MACK DAVID,
AL HOFFMAN and JERRY LIVINGSTON

TRUE LOVE'S KISS
from ENCHANTED

VIOLIN

Music by ALAN MENKEN
Lyrics by STEPHEN SCHWARTZ

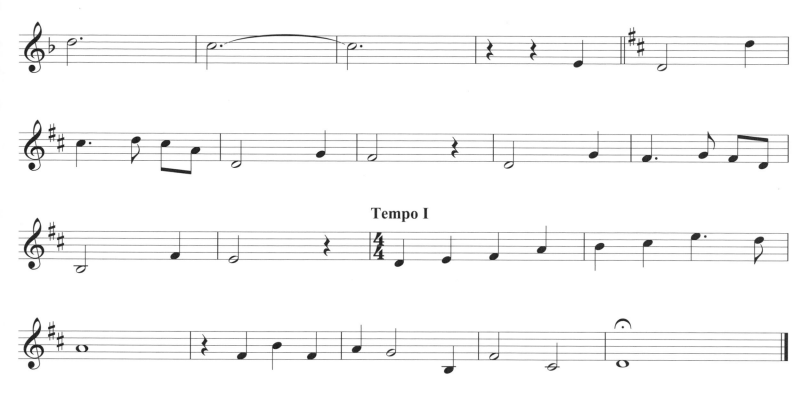

WESTWARD HO, THE WAGONS!

from WESTWARD HO, THE WAGONS!

Words by TOM BLACKBURN
Music by GEORGE BRUNS

WE BELONG TOGETHER

from TOY STORY 3

VIOLIN

Music and Lyrics by
RANDY NEWMAN

WHEN I SEE AN ELEPHANT FLY
from DUMBO

Words by NED WASHINGTON
Music by OLIVER WALLACE

WE KNOW THE WAY
from MOANA

VIOLIN

Music by OPETAIA FOA'I
Lyrics by OPETAIA FOA'I
and LIN-MANUEL MIRANDA

Moderately

A WHALE OF A TALE
from 20,000 LEAGUES UNDER THE SEA

Violin

Words and Music by NORMAN GIMBEL
and AL HOFFMAN

WE'RE ALL IN THIS TOGETHER

from HIGH SCHOOL MUSICAL

Violin

Words and Music by MATTHEW GERRARD
and ROBBIE NEVIL

WHISTLE WHILE YOU WORK
from SNOW WHITE AND THE SEVEN DWARFS

Words by LARRY MOREY
Music by FRANK CHURCHILL

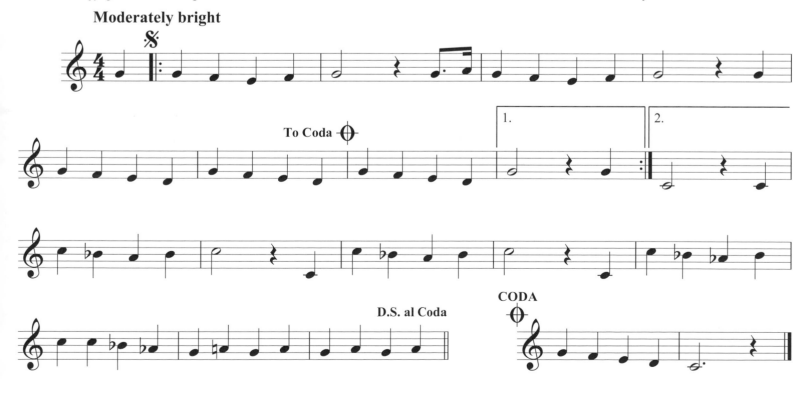

WHEN SHE LOVED ME

from TOY STORY 2

VIOLIN

Music and Lyrics by
RANDY NEWMAN

Tenderly, very freely

WHEN YOU WISH UPON A STAR
from PINOCCHIO

Violin

Words by NED WASHINGTON
Music by LEIGH HARLINE

Moderately

WHEN WILL MY LIFE BEGIN?

from TANGLED

VIOLIN

Music by ALAN MENKEN
Lyrics by GLENN SLATER

WITH A SMILE AND A SONG

from SNOW WHITE AND THE SEVEN DWARFS

Words by LARRY MOREY
Music by FRANK CHURCHILL

WHO'S AFRAID OF THE BIG BAD WOLF?

from THREE LITTLE PIGS

VIOLIN

Words and Music by
FRANK CHURCHILL
Additional Lyric by ANN RONELL

Moderately, in 2

WINNIE THE POOH
from THE MANY ADVENTURES OF WINNIE THE POOH

Violin

Words and Music by RICHARD M. SHERMAN
and ROBERT B. SHERMAN

Tenderly

A WHOLE NEW WORLD

from ALADDIN

VIOLIN

Music by ALAN MENKEN
Lyrics by TIM RICE

THE WONDERFUL THING ABOUT TIGGERS

Violin

from THE MANY ADVENTURES OF WINNIE THE POOH

Words and Music by RICHARD M. SHERMAN
and ROBERT B. SHERMAN

YO HO

(A Pirate's Life for Me)

from Disney Parks' Pirates of the Caribbean attraction

Words by XAVIER ATENCIO
Music by GEORGE BRUNS

THEME FROM ZORRO
from the Television Series

Words by NORMAN FOSTER
Music by GEORGE BRUNS

Moderately, in 2

WRITTEN IN THE STARS

from AIDA

VIOLIN

Music by ELTON JOHN
Lyrics by TIM RICE

YOU CAN FLY! YOU CAN FLY! YOU CAN FLY!

Violin

from PETER PAN

Words by SAMMY CAHN
Music by SAMMY FAIN

YOU ARE THE MUSIC IN ME

from HIGH SCHOOL MUSICAL 2

VIOLIN

Words and Music by
JAMIE HOUSTON

Moderately fast Rock

YOU'LL BE IN MY HEART

(Pop Version)
from TARZAN™

Violin

Words and Music by
PHIL COLLINS

CODA

YOU'RE WELCOME
from MOANA

VIOLIN

Music and Lyrics by
LIN-MANUEL MIRANDA

ZIP-A-DEE-DOO-DAH

from SONG OF THE SOUTH

Words by RAY GILBERT
Music by ALLIE WRUBEL

Brightly

ZERO TO HERO
from HERCULES

VIOLIN

Music by ALAN MENKEN
Lyrics by DAVID ZIPPEL

YOU'VE GOT A FRIEND IN ME

from TOY STORY

VIOLIN

Music and Lyrics by
RANDY NEWMAN

Easy Shuffle